# THE
# GREAT
## PHILOSOPHERS:
## SOCRATES, PLATO & ARISTOTLE

Ancient Greece | 5th Grade Biography | Children's Biographies

**DISSECTED LIVES**
auto biographies

First Edition, 2019

Published in the United States by Speedy Publishing LLC, 40 E Main Street, Newark, Delaware 19711 USA.

© 2019 Dissected Lives Books, an imprint of Speedy Publishing LLC

Dissected Lives Books are available at special discounts when purchased in bulk for industrial and sales-promotional use. For details contact our Special Sales Team at Speedy Publishing LLC, 40 E Main Street, Newark, Delaware 19711 USA. Telephone (888) 248-4521 Fax: (210) 519-4043. www.speedybookstore.com

10 9 8 7 6 * 5 4 3 2 1

Print Edition: 9781541950863
Digital Edition: 9781541952669

*See the world in pictures. Build your knowledge in style.*
https://www.speedypublishing.com/

# CONTENTS

Socrates, Plato, and Aristotle are the most well-know of the ancient Greek philosophers. The profound thinking and unique ideas from these three men greatly impacted our believes about government, morality, and education. In this book, we will discuss the lives of these three ancient Greek philosophers and their contributions to modern society.

SOCRATES

PLATO

ARISTOTLE

# WHAT IS PHILOSOPHY?

Philosophy is the study of the deep and important questions about human life. Philosophers, or people who study the various branches of philosophy, contemplate some thought-provoking questions, such as why we exist, what makes people inherently good or evil, and do our actions control out fate? They strive to find a balance between logic and emotions and faith.

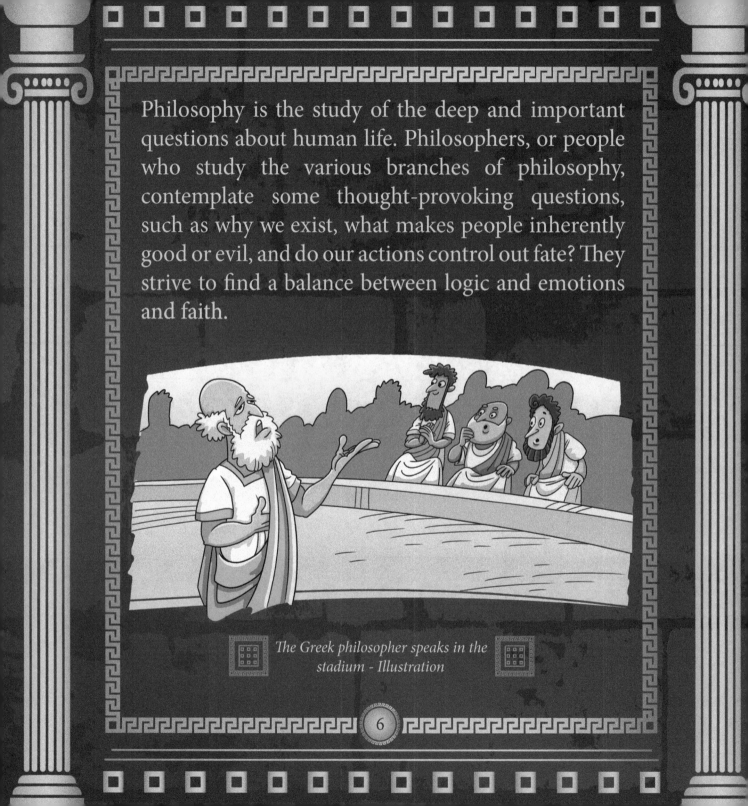

*The Greek philosopher speaks in the stadium - Illustration*

They study literature, the natural world, science, and human nature. They debate other philosophers. Additionally, philosophical issues can be found in all areas of study. We often find that the greatest philosophers are also doctors, mathematicians, teachers, writers, and scientists.

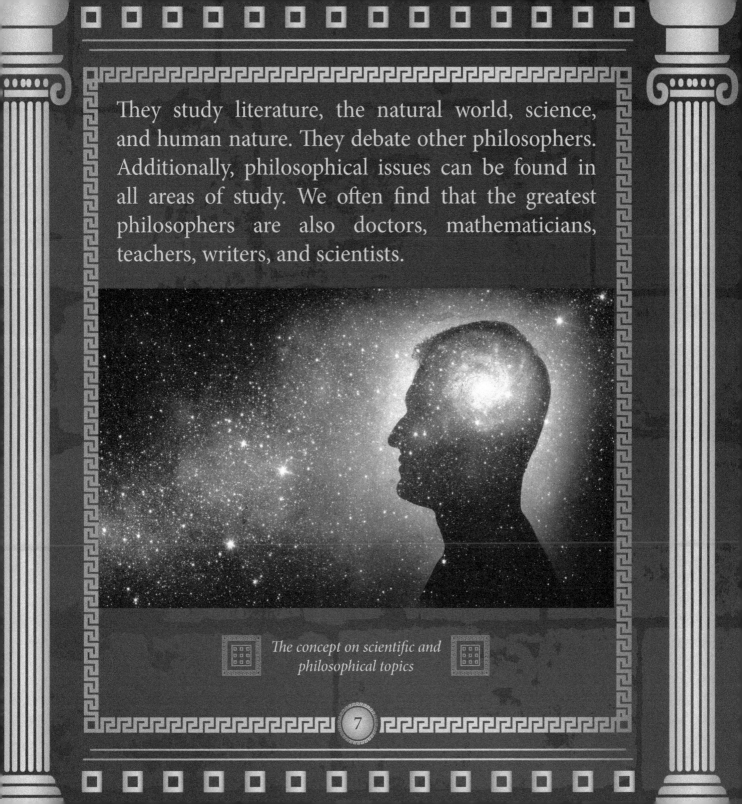

*The concept on scientific and philosophical topics*

# WHO WAS SOCRATES?

*Socrates an Ancient Greek Philosopher*

Socrates was an ancient Greek philosopher who lived from about 470 to 399 BC.

He was born in Athens, Greece, and historians think that he lived his entire live in that city, except for the brief time when he served as a soldier in the Greek military. Socrates was married and had three sons. Because his father was a stonemason—a person who cuts and carves stone—historians think that Socrates also trained to work as a stonemason. It doesn't appear that he kept this job for long. Instead of working, Socrates devoted his time to learning, reading, and discussing philosophical ideas. It is believed that his family was wealthy enough to allow Socrates the freedom to pursue his self-education.

The Acropolis of Athens,
Greece

# PUBLIC DEBATES

One of the activities that Socrates loved was exchanging philosophical ideas with others. He would meet with other scholars in public places, such as parks, and hold lively conversations under shady trees.

*Socrates and his students*

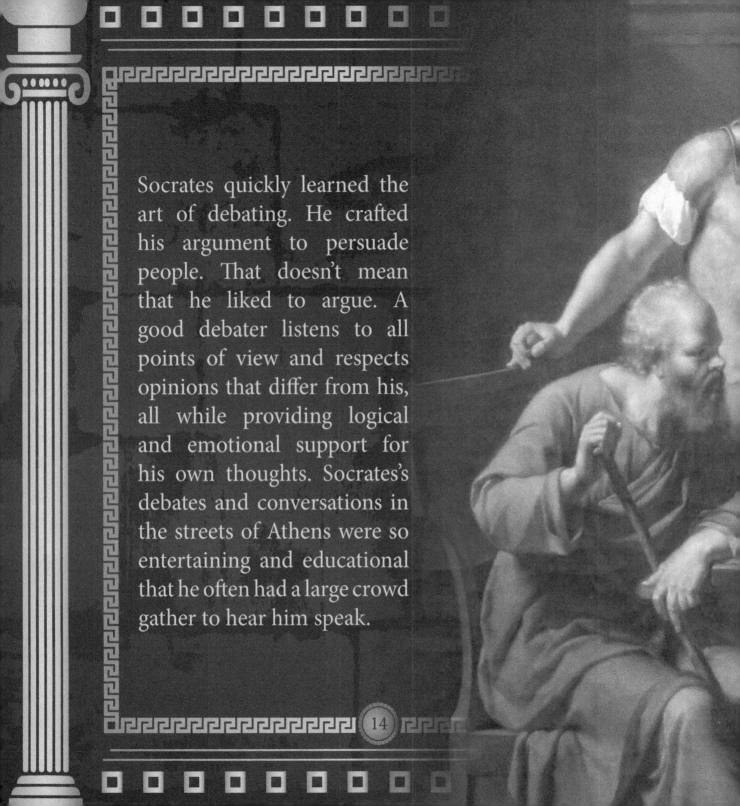

Socrates quickly learned the art of debating. He crafted his argument to persuade people. That doesn't mean that he liked to argue. A good debater listens to all points of view and respects opinions that differ from his, all while providing logical and emotional support for his own thoughts. Socrates's debates and conversations in the streets of Athens were so entertaining and educational that he often had a large crowd gather to hear him speak.

# THE TEACHINGS OF
# SOCRATES

Unlike most other ancient philosophers, Socrates did not write down his teachings and idea. Thankfully, others did.

*Alcibiades Being Taught by Socrates*

Many of his devoted followers, including Plato, who we will discuss later in this book, took thorough notes when attending Socrates's talks. These notes have survived through the ages to give us a glimpse of concepts and ideas of this great philosopher. In addition, many of the philosophers that came after Socrates used his teachings as a basis for their own writings. This also helps us to understand the mind of Socrates.

Socrates teaching

# THE SOCRATIC METHOD

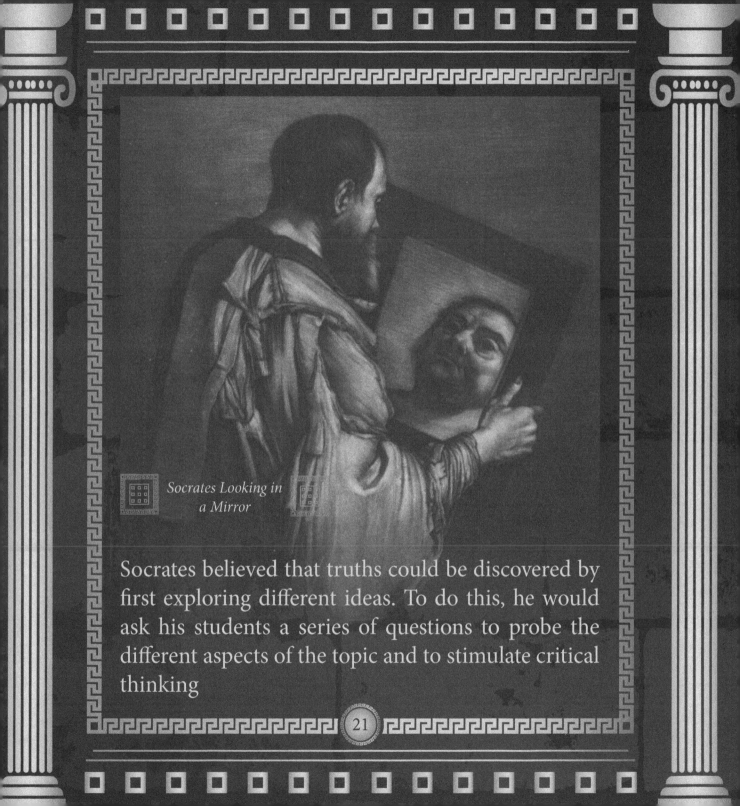

*Socrates Looking in a Mirror*

Socrates believed that truths could be discovered by first exploring different ideas. To do this, he would ask his students a series of questions to probe the different aspects of the topic and to stimulate critical thinking

Through dialog and debate, he could discover basic, universal beliefs that form the foundation of thought. From there, Socrates posed various questions to gauge how those beliefs remain consistent or differ in other situations. The questions he asked were all purposefully open-ended questions that forced the student to formulate their own response rather than recite a fact. The Socratic Method is still a popular teaching tool today and is common in many university classes.

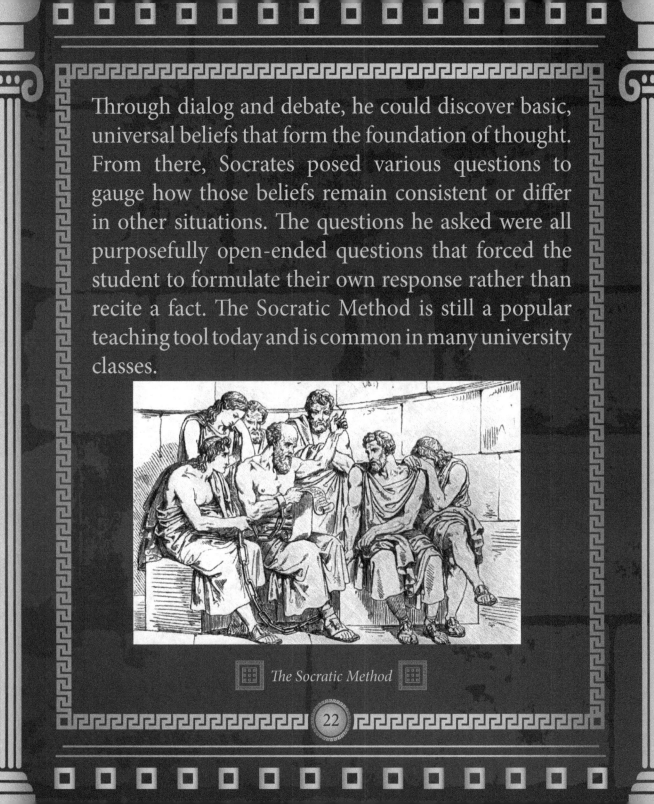

The Socratic Method

# THE TRIAL AND EXECUTION OF SOCRATES

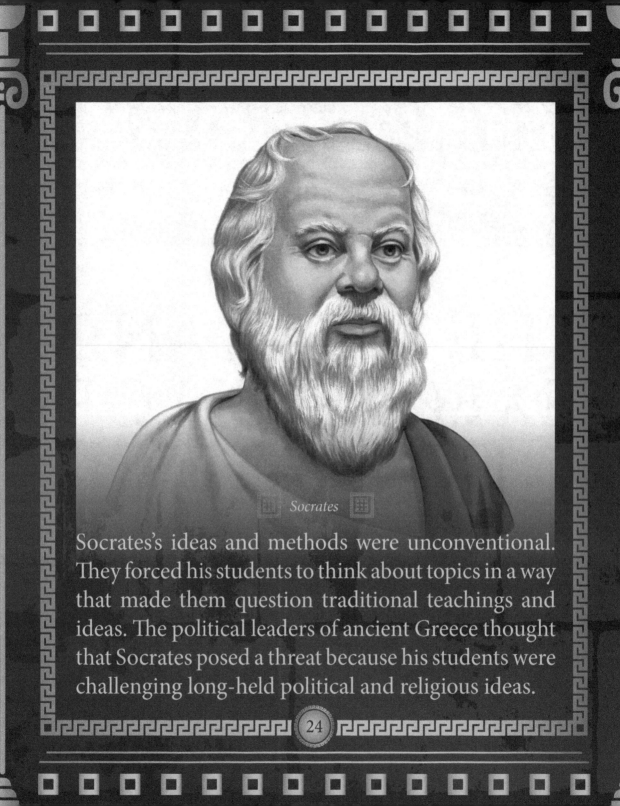

*Socrates*

Socrates's ideas and methods were unconventional. They forced his students to think about topics in a way that made them question traditional teachings and ideas. The political leaders of ancient Greece thought that Socrates posed a threat because his students were challenging long-held political and religious ideas.

In 399 BC, Socrates was arrested and stood trial on charges that he was corrupting the minds of the youth of Athens and that he did not believe in the gods. He was found guilty and sentenced to death by poisoning.

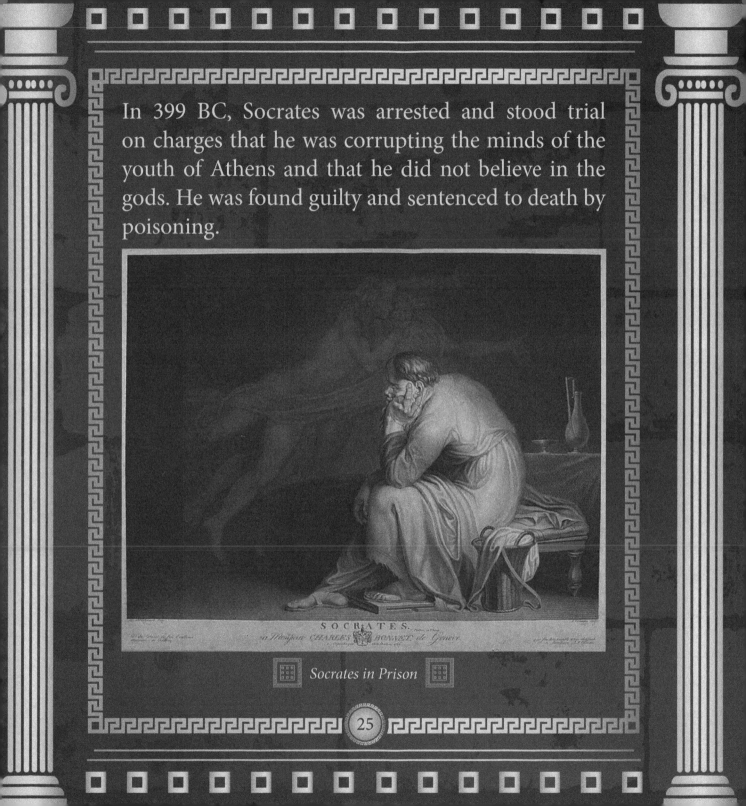

Socrates in Prison

Socrates was made to drink a cup full of poison hemlock, a deadly poison.

# WHO WAS PLATO?

*Plato*

Plato, who lived from about 428 to 348 BC, was a student of Socrates.

Like his teacher, Plato became one of the greatest and most-influential of the ancient Greek philosophers.

*Socrates And Plato*

Born and raised in Athens, Plato came from a wealthy family and had ambitions to enter into politics. The arrest, trial, and execution of his beloved teacher, Socrates, however, deeply affected Plato. He blamed the political system in Athens for Socrates's death and vowed that he could not join such an institution. Instead, Plato decided to leave Athens to experience different cultures. He traveled throughout Greece, Italy, and Egypt.

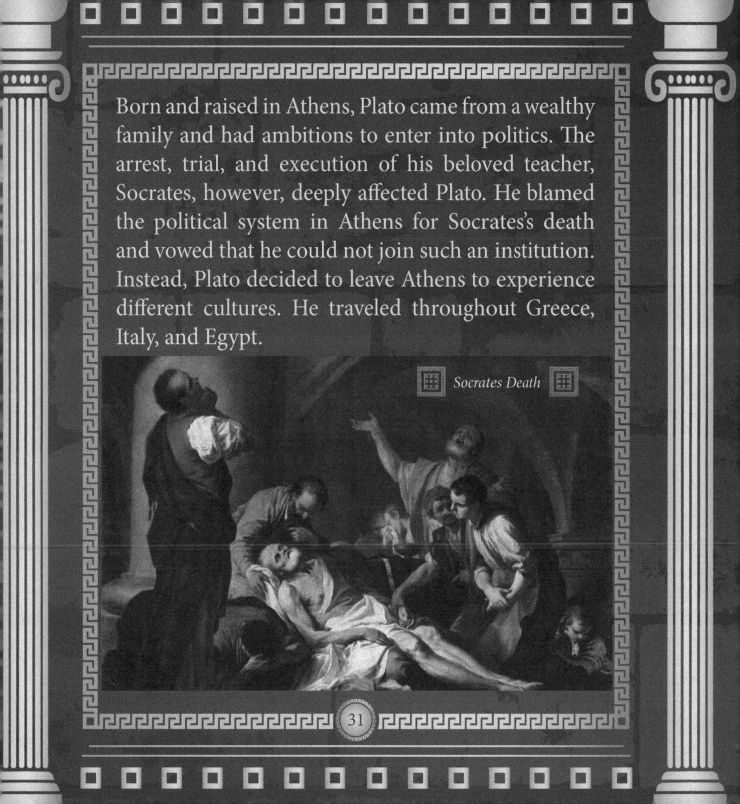

*Socrates Death*

# PLATO'S
# ACADEMY

Plato returned to Athens and, in 387 BC, he founded the Academy of Athens.

At his Academy, he taught students a variety of subjects, from mathematics and science to law and philosophy. Located in a grove of olive trees just outside the walls of Athens, the Academy was named for the classic Athenian hero, Akademos. Plato's school was so influential that today, the term Academy is synonymous with an educational facility.

The ancient site of Plato's Academy.
Ruins of the Square Peristyle

Historians point to Plato's Academy as the forerunner of today's universities of higher learning. Plato was very proud of his school and taught there for the rest of his life. The Academy attracted many brilliant students, among them was Aristotle, who we will discuss later in this book.

# PLATO THE
# WRITER

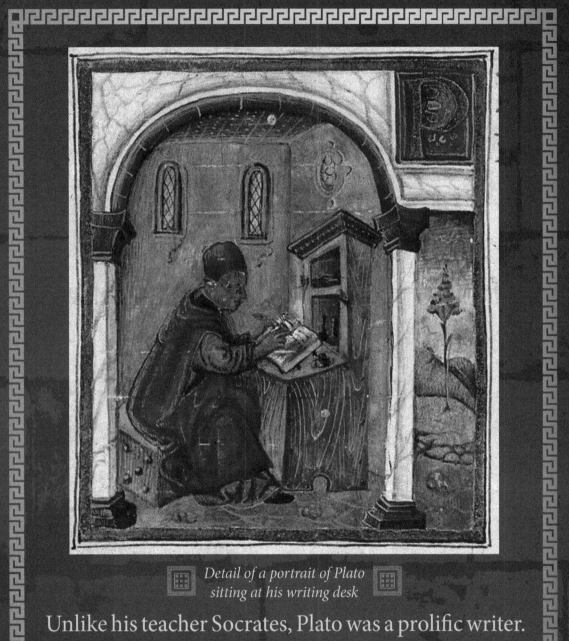

*Detail of a portrait of Plato
sitting at his writing desk*

Unlike his teacher Socrates, Plato was a prolific writer.

He produced an impressive volume of writings on a wide range of topics, including politics, geometry, ethics, and love. Many of Plato's works contain references to Socrates and his teachings so historians know that much of Plato's thinking was inspired by his former teacher.

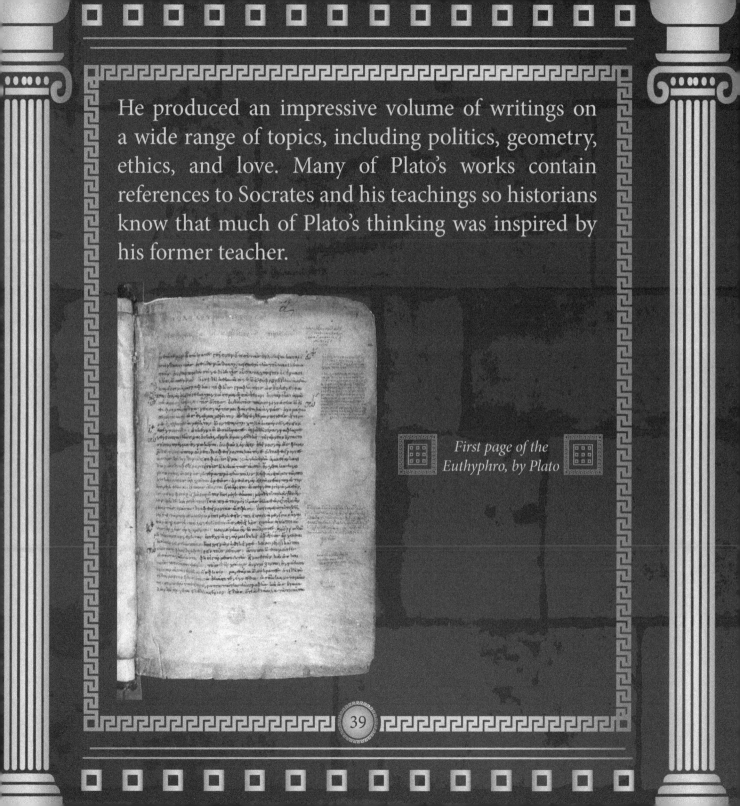

*First page of the Euthyphro, by Plato*

One example of this is Plato's most famous work, Republic, written in 380 BC. Republic is written like a dialog between himself and Socrates and is one of the most important works in political theory and philosophy. This book is still being studied and discussed today.

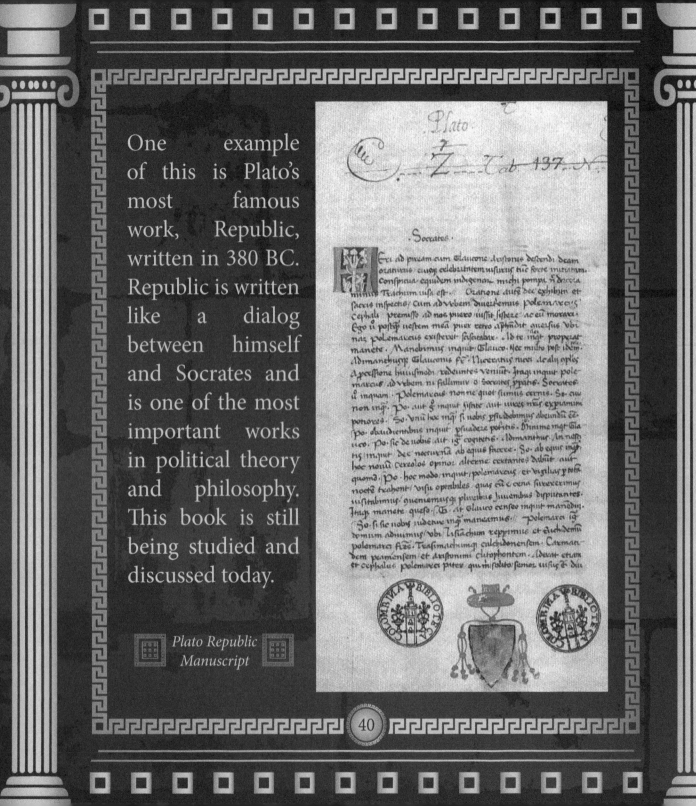

*Plato Republic Manuscript*

# PLATO'S
# DEATH

Plato died 348 BC, on the day of his birthday. Accounts vary about how he died, but he was a very old man, in his eighties. One story says he died while attending a wedding feast. Another suggests that Plato died peacefully in his sleep while a young girl played softly on her flute.

PLATO
RAPH. SANCT. Vrb. pinxit in aed Vatic.

Plato

His death was much less dramatic than Socrates, but still had a profound impact on many of his former students, including Aristotle.

*Plato statue, the Ancient Greek Philosopher*

# WHO WAS ARISTOTLE?

*Aristotle*

Aristotle, who lived from 384 to 322 BC, was the son of a physician from Stagira, located in the northeastern part of Greece.

In fact, Aristotle's father was the doctor for the King of Macedonia, located north of Greece. A great scholar and thinker, Aristotle left home when he was still a teenager to attend Plato's Academy in Athens. There, he further developed his philosophical understandings and began writing his important ideas and thoughts.

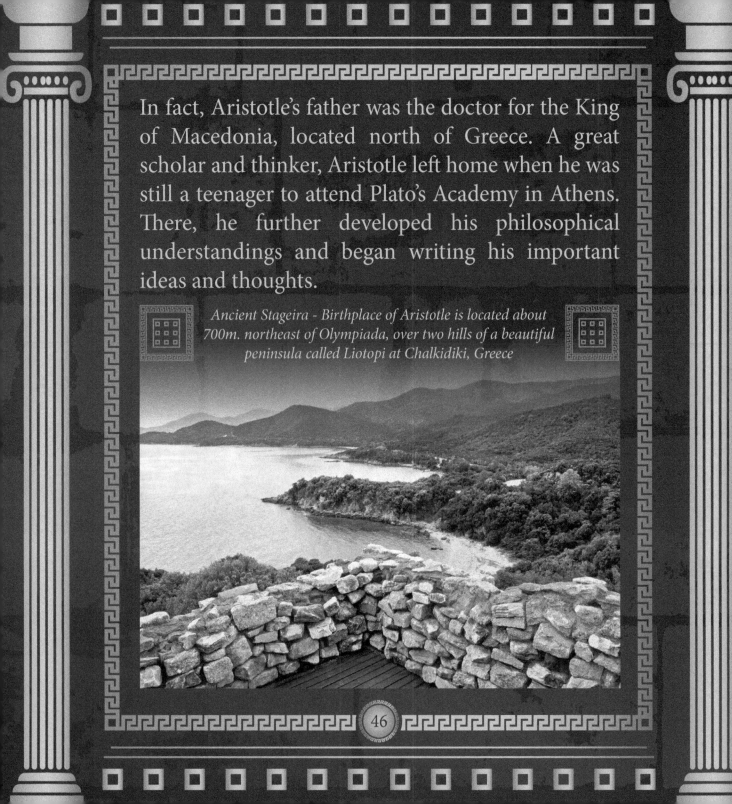

*Ancient Stageira - Birthplace of Aristotle is located about 700m. northeast of Olympiada, over two hills of a beautiful peninsula called Liotopi at Chalkidiki, Greece*

Like his teacher, Plato, Aristotle was a voracious writer and his works provide us with a catalog of ancient Greek knowledge.

*A representation of Aristotle and Plato discussing philosophy in a garden*

# ARISTOTLE AND ALEXANDER THE GREAT

When Plato died in 348 BC, Aristotle left the Academy in Athens. For a time, he traveled to different cities in Greece and Macedonia. His father even helped him get a job tutoring the son of the Macedonian King.

*Skopje Main Square City Macedonia*

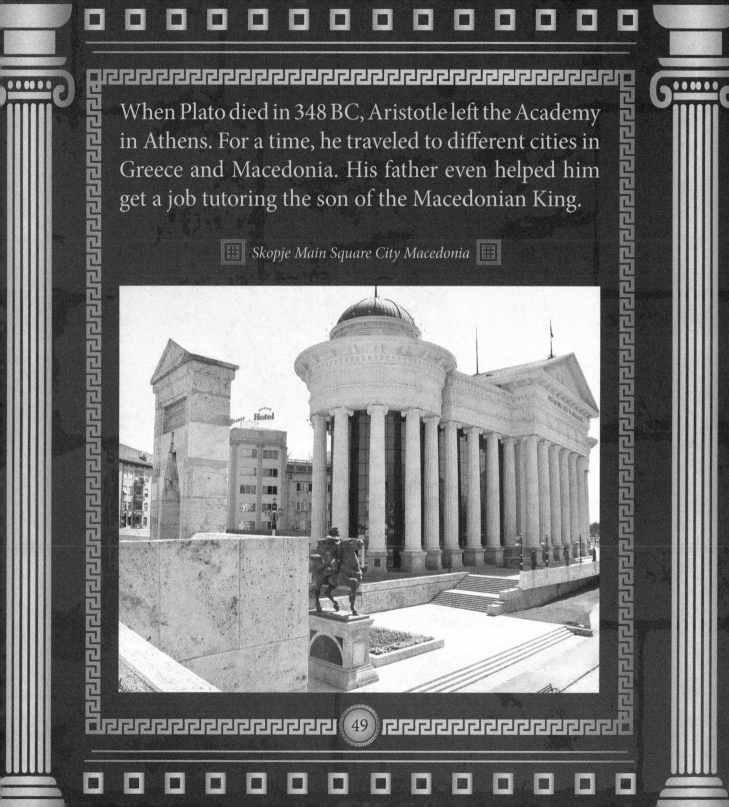

This young prince was none other than the famous leader and military genius Alexander the Great. Young Alexander was tutored by Aristotle until he was about 16 years old, then ascended the throne at the age of 20. Considered one of the most successful military minds in history, Alexander the Great expanded the Macedonian empire through a series of spectacular military victories.

*Aristotle and his pupil Alexander the Great*

The instruction he received from Aristotle helped Alexander the Great achieve success.

*Alexander the Great*

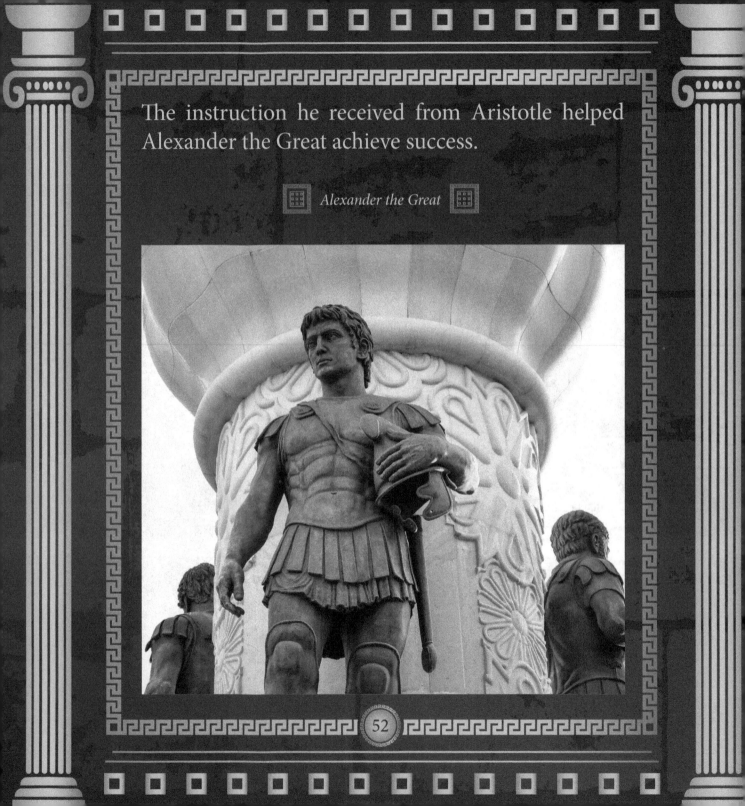

# ARISTOTLE'S OWN SCHOOL

Aristotle eventually returned to Athens. In 335 BC, he opened his own school there, called the Lyceum, which competed against Plato's Academy.

*Aristotle Lycaeum or Lyceum was a temple dedicated to Apollo Lyceus. It was best known for the Peripatetic school of philosophy founded by Aristotle*

*Aristotle at his writing-desk*

Like Plato, Aristotle spent the remainder of his life working at his school, teaching and writing. What made the Lyceum different than the Academy was that Aristotle didn't just focus his teachings on philosophy, mathematics, and politics.

He included a wide range of topics, including history, astronomy, zoology, and biology. Often, Aristotle presented the lectures to his students as he strolled back and forth on the Lyceum's peripatos, or covered porch. Soon, his students became known as Peripatetics.

*Historia Animalium, one of Aristotle's books on biology*

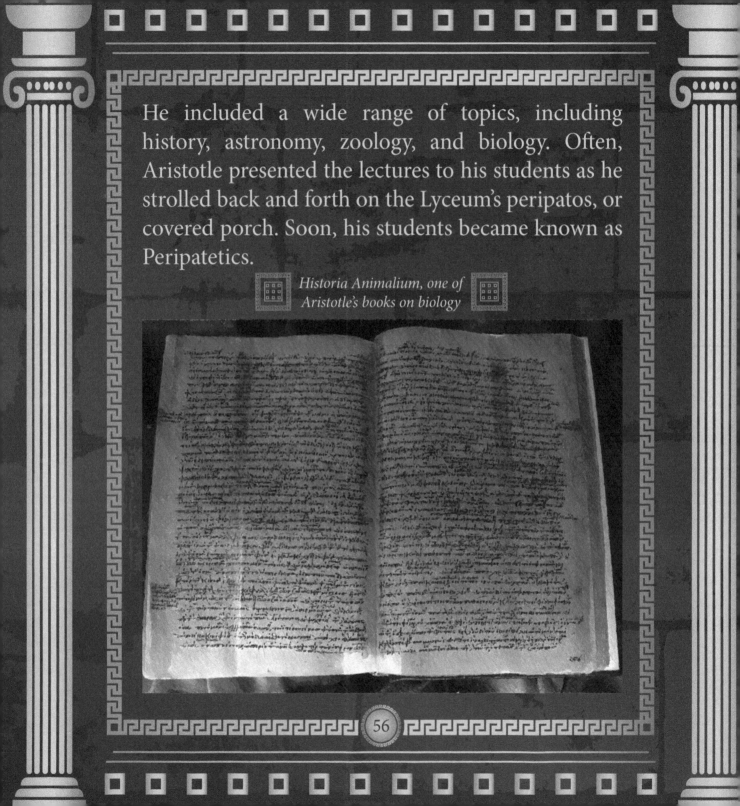

# THE LOGIC OF
# ARISTOTLE

Aristotle has been called the father of logic, using reasoning to uncover truths about the world. He developed the syllogism, a form of logical argument using known information to deduce unknown information. A syllogism starts with a major truism, or premise, followed by a second, lesser premise.

*Statue of Aristotle a great greek philosopher*

From these, the conclusion is reached. A classic example of this is called the Barbara Syllogism, which argues: All men are mortal. Socrates is a man. Therefore, Socrates is mortal. This basis for logical reasoning helped to inform scientific study.

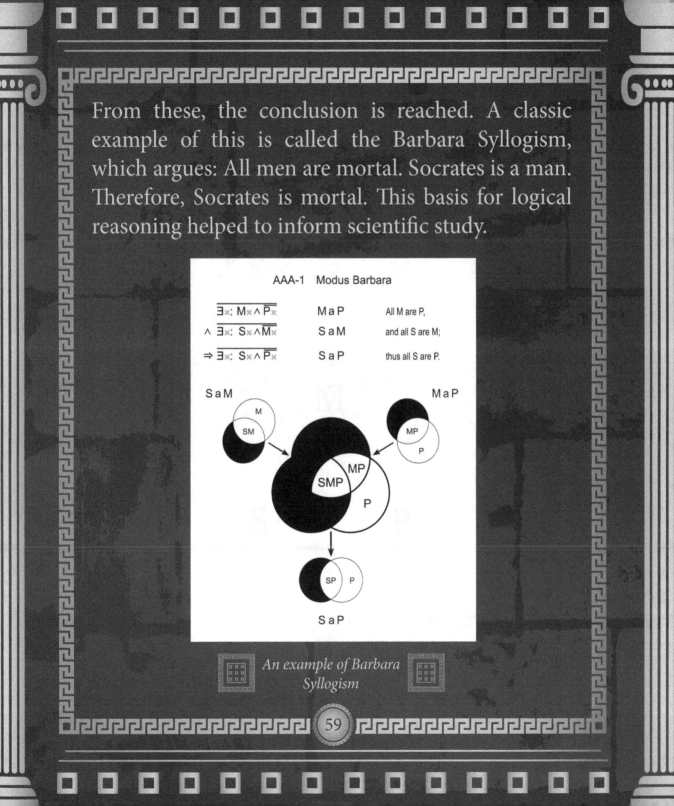

*An example of Barbara Syllogism*

# ARISTOTLE'S WRITINGS

Aristotle left behind more than two thousand documents that included his lecture notes and his personal observations, both covering numerous topics. His interests were broad and diverse. He studied geography, physics, anatomy, and meteorology, as well as poetry, literature, and rhetoric.

*Aristotle, Physics*
*The beginning of the "Physics" in an incunable printed at Venice decorated with hand-painted miniatures. New York, Pierpont Morgan Library*

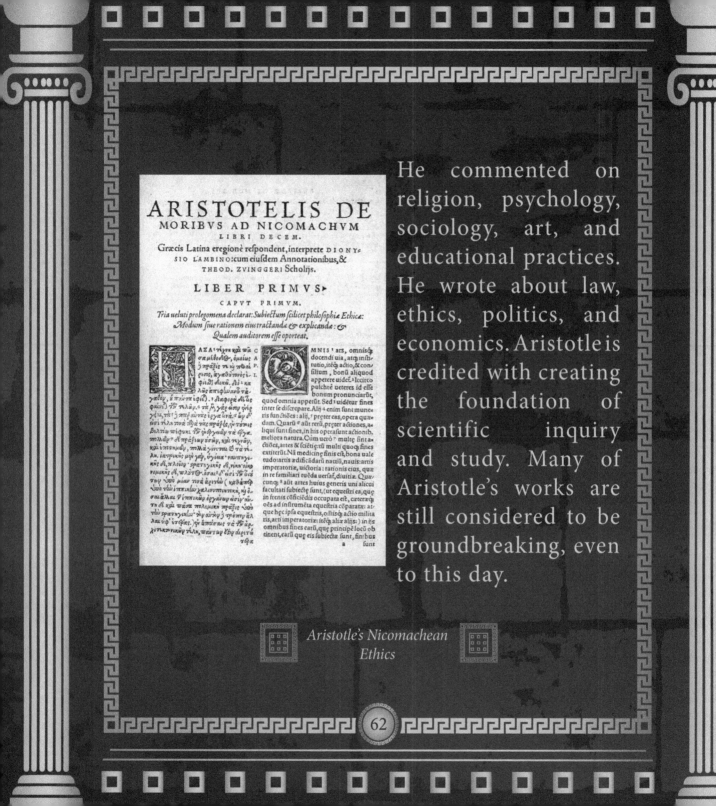

He commented on religion, psychology, sociology, art, and educational practices. He wrote about law, ethics, politics, and economics. Aristotle is credited with creating the foundation of scientific inquiry and study. Many of Aristotle's works are still considered to be groundbreaking, even to this day.

*Aristotle's Nicomachean Ethics*

# THE DEATH OF ARISTOTLE

In 323 BC, Aristotle retired from teaching at his Lyceum and moved to the quiet Greek island of Chalcis. He contracted a stomach ailment and died the following year. His scholarly work was the standard by which other academic research was based. It took the next two thousand years before scholars were able to make advances on Aristotle's work in zoology, logic, and more. His work even formed the basis for the work done by Roman and Caliphate scholars. During the Middle Ages, translations of Aristotle's writings dominated teachings throughout all of Europe.

*City of Chalkis, Euboea, Greece, aerial view*

*Statue of Aristotle a great*
*greek philosopher*

Socrates

# Summary

The influence of these three ancient Greek philosophers, Socrates, Plato, and Aristotle, extends from antiquity to modern times. They pioneered the study of philosophy and set the stage for politics, education, law, ethics, science, and mathematics knowledge that, in turn, led to modern thought and society.

Learning about the lives of these three Greek philosophers will help you understand the importance of the culture of ancient Greece.

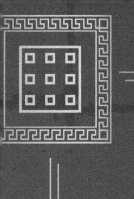

Visit

BABY PROFESSOR
EDUCATION KIDS

www.BabyProfessorBooks.com
to download Free Baby Professor eBooks and view our
catalog of new and exciting Children's Books

9 781541 950863